ON WH
MOU

Other Books
by Martyn Crucefix

Beneath Tremendous Rain

ON WHISTLER MOUNTAIN

Martyn Crucefix

SINCLAIR-STEVENSON

First published in Great Britain 1994
by Sinclair-Stevenson
an imprint of Reed Consumer Books Ltd
Michelin House, 81 Fulham Road, London SW3 6RB
and Auckland, Melbourne, Singapore and Toronto

ISBN 1 85619 333 0

A CIP catalogue record for this title
is available from the British Library

Typeset by Deltatype Ltd, Ellesmere Port, Cheshire
Printed and bound in Great Britain
by Cox & Wyman Ltd, Reading, Berkshire

for Louise

Acknowledgements

Some of these poems, or versions of them, have appeared in *Acumen, Ambit, Bête Noire, The Bound Spiral, Critical Quarterly, The Green Book, The London Review of Books, Oxford Poetry, Poetry Review, Poetry Wales, The Rialto, Sheffield Thursday, Staple* and *The Times Literary Supplement*.

'Prelude to an Unwritten Sequence' appeared in the anthology *Affirming Flame* (Community Projects Foundation, 1989), under the title 'Horlogerie'.

Several of these poems were included in a collection short-listed in the Poetry Business Competition 1992. 'The Greek Gifts' appeared in the Poetry Business anthology *Greek Gifts* (Smith-Doorstop, 1992).

'At The Mountjoy Hotel' came second in the Arvon/Observer Poetry Competition 1991 and appeared in a limited edition pamphlet from Enitharmon Press in 1993. The poem was completed with the help of a Hawthornden Fellowship in the summer of 1991.

'Moths' was a prizewinner in the National Poetry Competition 1990. 'Grain's Gill' was a prizewinner in the Cardiff International Poetry Competition 1992 and appears in *The Blue Nose Poetry Anthology* (Blue Nose Press, 1993) with the poem 'Afterwards'.

'On Whistler Mountain' won joint first prize in the Sheffield Thursday Poetry Competition, 1993

Contents

Prelude to an Unwritten Sequence

I come from a line of clockmakers, refugees
from the massacre of St Bartholomew's Day.
They came to Spitalfields, the Clockmakers' Company,
to the anger of natives whose curtains
lifted on strangers from across the sea.
Settling with the look of death upon them,
their voices rang alien in unfamiliar streets.

Days marked by the knocking of the family clock,
they laboured long hours at each mechanism
to align spring and movement, spindle and dial.
And when the work was done, a sinuous snake
would take possession of that house and time
slid amongst bright cogwheels, began to unwind
the hurried stamp of their frightened hearts.

But these things are obscured in me –
the Register of Aliens, French Christian names,
sheep's head brass and red lacquer bracket,
their church buildings, bright apprentice boys,
shop fronts, street cries. The only reminder
is this watch on my wrist, where my days blink.
They would not recognise its digital squeak.
Yet for their sake and for my own, what I
want is time enough for me to recover
whatever pieces I can, aligned, unwinding
words to tell hours, how they crowd upon us,
how my blood beats down this line of clockmakers.

Part One

At The Mountjoy Hotel

I

Let me tell you – lunchtime boozing
never agreed, but he gets them in anyway.
"Who doesn't?" he shrugs.

And which one of you will blame him?
Beached in this unrelieved morgue,
this market town, this middle-England,

the thick end of a dozen miles from Coventry.
You see – the Hotel's class but he hates
the maids, their gloss and preen, their "Sir"

and "Yes, sir", no matter how he treats them.
They're like those white peppermint chunks
that get dropped in urinals: pissed on

they pump out a perfume designed to please
but which snags his nose.
Even so, he's already chatted

the specially simpering one,
her complexion pitted like a strawberry.
I know now. I am more scared to lose

my home than my virginity.
When I told Mum that, she didn't laugh.
Now we're here. At The Mountjoy Hotel.

II

And this should be my best day.
No, I don't mean just to look my best.
I've tried to be rid of silly illusions –

but then I get so excited.
So, fair play and all that.
I knew you'd not be first to cast

a stone, in fact, sympathise,
as he waits for a call that'll probably
never come, to troubleshoot this hardware

that somebody else should've wedded
and bedded three weeks ago.
The Mountjoy then, dancing graceless

attendance till Sunday noon at least.
As I said – a beery lunch leaves him
slack in the lobby's creaking leather,

zooming guests for a wedding, who trail
off the by-pass, same two names
ringing at the desk, the Hotel filling

for a farce he knows will open
the stable door long after the pair of them
have screwed each other senseless.

III

His'n'hers. He sees arrivals offering
their most adult glove,
their hypocritical best, as they jerk off

the froth of meet and greet in the lobby.
Sees the groom's old money: bony, moon-faces,
ancients, spindly, from private wards.

The bride's blood with that ruddy, cock-
sure, club-swinging, poorly-cut swagger
in throat and limb

he'll recognise one day with warmth
(though long after he's forgotten all this)
as his own true inheritance.

I'm the reason people have come here.
No. I should say "we". Our reason's to tell them
we're happy, to have them share it.

It's not envy. Now — don't misunderstand.
He's more disposable than he can spend.
They play the blood-stained family game.

He despises them, their Holier-than-thou
handshakes and clinches and the strawberry-
faced maid who flaps to help them.

IV

He needs air. He takes it.
Standing on the Hotel steps, dizzied
by the sensation, the familiar whizz-bang

of brilliant daylight exploding
over his beer-wretched eyeballs.
Moments ago, in the lobby's cool gloom,

they were foetuses, pickled, calm and easy,
screwed tight in a jar.
Now he wakes them with the Mountjoy's

brazen patriotism, the Union flag quivers,
headlong on a pole, whitewashed,
piercing, bull's-eye, the crew-cut lawn.

More strength in the air since breakfast.
He's bored. Taking steps two at a time,
he heads for the High Street.

Don't worry! It's OK.
If the call comes through and they can't hit him
at the Hotel, he carries a pager.

Don't think he's no good at his job.
He deserves his screw — which I'd guess
is more than most of you.

V

Passing Oxfam, he double-takes the woman
at the till. It's his mother from years back
laughing at him as he struggles

with a skirt behind the secondhand rail.
He dives angrily at the door,
the old bell clanking, but this branch

is smaller than the place he knows
his mother still works. She looks up and smiles.
He rubs this rubbish from his eyes.

Mum says stand like a tailor's dummy.
Today, that's fine. Because her eyes are raw.
Because she's bitten her lip red.

Why do weddings make for all these tears?
There are sides to him I don't know.
Even some I don't like.

But I never wanted to marry myself.
On past *Ritz Video*, its rectangular harvest
the kind of imagination he has.

At the Shell Station,
he smiles to see a man — two men —
shake the drops from their petrol-guns.

VI

Smiles. Knows instinctively it's not
economy alone, the reason they do that.
Knows too, without checking –

everything is this clear –
that women don't do it. Reason's simple.
Anatomical. No prick to shake.

The feminine mind-set's unscrupulous,
lacks detail and finish, never focuses, spreads,
a delta, reeky stain on blotching paper.

Mum! Don't start up now.
Not tears. No! Please, Mum.
Oh! Now you've set me off.

There are only great men – imposers, achievers –
the strongest of women wrest control
over themselves, not others –

and most love it, perfume and prink it.
And he's right. Look – the living proof
as he gets back to the bottom

of the Mountjoy steps:
wedding guests mill at their starting traps.
A dismal, feminine, rivalry of hats.

VII

The wind begins to fill with rain.
The beery phlegm on his tongue's contempt
for the flurry of painted hands

on hair and heaving breasts
as the carefully calculated tilt of hats
gets smothered in an upsprouting

of ill-prepared umbrellas that clash.
Why bother, is what Debbie says.
Who needs this fashion parade? Shack up!

Just don't tell me you see each other
arm in arm on the aisle and better for it.
For being joined, not divided.

That love's an island in a sea of sharks.
I say: No. Love is what lies between us.
Oh God! she howls. So David's religious?

I say: what's religious about that?
From his bed, he views a painting on the wall.
A stringy spurt of black

from the Gallery of Robert Young (it says).
Reminds him of the sprout of his armpit hair.
Some pink strands enliven the black.

VIII

Now it's the flared scuff of a scrape
on the outside wing of his white Cavalier.
There is no scrape –

but just imagining it makes him mad.
There is Debbie. Her baby's bound to cry.
Sun's brightened in the window.

She's hungry. She's chewing the hymn-sheet.
Here's my darling. Now he's turning . . .
Art's only for those who find the real thing

too tough. He doesn't.
But this kind of wall-hanging's okay.
It sits on his consciousness, oil on water,

a mark that wants nothing much in response.
No smug inquiry about how to behave.
No snipe at success. No belly-ache

about duty, responsibility.
No whining voices wanting attention
for something that shows they want treatment.

That just puts human arse before elbow.
Worse — it's boring.
Art slumps against the real for support.

IX

Still no call. It's the worst of the job.
He's getting restless as you . . .
Flicks Gideon — suicide, lost faith, the lonely —

tosses it back for the no-hopers to come.
When I promise will anybody hear me?
I don't mean the congregation.

Debbie says she knows it's not true.
But aren't people who believe it all happy?
Now I'm here and I've never wondered.

I might come to church more often after this.
Think of standing here. Us two. Them all.
That roaring! It's pouring rain again.

Oh, God! The photographs! Make it sunny!
I'm sorry. Selfish. I meant not to be.
I will. Has everything changed?

Lonesome men marry.
They need that frequent release.
Women — though plenty of them don't know it yet —

need kids and kitchens.
CineMovies list *The Budding of Bree*,
"a young actress with sheer talent and lingerie".

X

He flicks the remote. Settles back
to a flashcard: CineMovies
don't cable that film till late at night.

You won't blame him, will you?
If he decides that sums this cowboy-run
country up? Where Big Brother,

the corporate socialists, pump your wallet
and slip you a ruse.
He showers for consolation.

Remembers how much he likes hotels:
same oat-meal colour from wall-to-wall,
from ceiling to floor. Easy on the eye.

Likes to leave towels in a heap on the floor.
The miracle of someone paid to pick them up!
Stepping out, he thinks

how he likes the little free bath-foam
and shampoo bottles like blue chess-pieces
with their spherical tops.

This is a lifetime's smiling.
Hurry! Hurry up!
I want to sit quiet with him in the car.

XI

Mirror. Scratch the itch
of dissatisfaction out. High cheekbones.
Thicker hair. Not a bad looker.

And he gets at least his fair share.
Reconsiders the bitch, the strawberry maid,
sees her flapping in the lobby this morning.

Thinks of the be-hatted marriage-brigade.
He can hear their unlikely promises,
the rain booming on the church roof.

None of the hats have turned to yawn
through leaded diamonds, not bored by virtue
for today at least.

The men count down keys in their pockets.
He sees the photographs rained-out, the cars
back to the Mountjoy smelling

of rain-soaked sleeves – now drinks – gossip –
later, the reception – her friends –
all single women –

every one brimming with vapid romance
and too much gin. Something worth the wait!
He hits the TV. Sleeps.

XII

I went out like a light.
When Mum said rest now, I slept the sleep
I lost last night. It's a long day,

she said. But then I dreamed of the night.
Although not very clearly.
Now imagine the complex web of the Hotel

spread around him as he sleeps:
nets of electricity and central-heating,
plumbing systems carefully sling him.

Imagine the interdependence of weight
and load, the brief shift and borrow of air
in this big bellows as doors press shut

at one corridor-end and lifts come precisely
to rest at level after level, their doors
sighing open. Imagine

the human systems of laundry
the service cleaners, chains of command,
the kitchens ready for his least whim,

shoe-shine, desk clerk, the florist,
the service man for the pool in his overalls.
Now imagine why he likes hotels.

XIII

Awake. The reception thunders
in the Queen's Room. On his way there,
the strawberry maid pauses to cut him dead.

Predatory, a little peeved,
he crashes the unguarded wedding-party
to find the food's all gone.

A familiar scene. You'd know it well.
In one corner, a console flashing coloured lights
at the milling few who jig and wriggle

in approximate beat to the music.
Away to one side, he guesses
the day's heroine in a leopard-print dress.

She has a full mouth and short dark hair.
A virgin for sure. He forgets he was wrong
and tries to decide which of the bucks

she'll be punctured by.
He smirks at the gauche, the students
of Gideon, the seriousness, shoulder-pads,

the peacock-show of middle-England,
youth snuffed out at the sound of a bell
and middle age dropped in the drum-beat.

XIV

Here are the bride and her bridegroom.
Husband and wife. I've done it.
Often. This dance. But never imagined

these aching feet. Soon we'll go to bed.
I've thought of that too.
He sits at the bar. Knows no-one.

Doesn't want to be known.
He's overridden enough rebuffs to know,
when boy meets girl, the nettle that sprouts

between them is sex and must be grasped –
yes, by the man first if she's timorous –
or it'll hurt them both

and nothing will grow there besides.
There's nothing else on his mind
when a less than delicate hand,

used to hard work, taps his arm
and asks for a drink. The strawberry maid –
in civvies that do less to flatter her figure

than her uniform. She's swallowed her pride.
As he sees her smile, he thinks
later that night he'll come in her mouth.

XV

I'd read books. But they were novels.
I'd seen it on film. Their slow-motion
made what we did seem too fast.

How long does it usually take?
I shouldn't have asked him that, I think.
We left the Mountjoy early, left them

all dancing. Mum finally let herself loose,
a proper cry and Dad was shaking
hands with everybody – even me.

I could tell he was afraid to hold me.
Then a fast drive to this other Hotel.
I wished we'd done it already – though

I couldn't tell him as we'd agreed to wait.
I felt knackered. I knew too well
how he'd been looking forward. Me too.

He was big even before he took his pants off.
I couldn't look. I couldn't not.
I opened my arms, relaxed everything for him.

I was so unpractised.
Excited when he came.
And then he said he was sorry.

XVI

He wakes late. Her smell on his palm.
She's left him a note.
A name, number, effusive pleas.

It was good. A change. The woman
he sleeps with is lazy in bed – as if she
thought the act was more than itself,

16

less important than the state of mind
that provokes it. Though he'd not say that.
He'd try tossing out "frigid",

then play it by ear, taking care
to dump the suspicion that nothing
he does really turns her on.

On nights he's out of the house,
she amuses herself. He's smelt it sometimes
through her pungent soap . . .

The memory shifts him.
The shower boils him red.
Two more sodden towels on the floor.

You sleep so quietly. David. David.
Remember? This is our honeymoon.
Wake up. I want to do it again.

XVII

Can't risk seeing the strawberry girl again.
He leaves the Hotel and since he's scouted
the town, he turns the other way.

Thinks if there's no call now, he'll bolt.
A churchyard where yesterday's
marriage-farce took place.

He watches grey-hairs leave morning service.
Now — let's be clear. Churchgoing
is no habit with him, but everybody's

tempted once in a while. He walks up,
twists the bull-nose ring
and taps out a few steps and sees

yesterday's couple (halfway to Heathrow
by now) vowing fidelity
till they're blue in the face.

Gate Seventeen. British Airways. To Athens.
He sees a child on a woman's lap.
She has dropped her coloured rag-book.

She prefers to suck the printed hymn-sheet.
She loves the embossed lettering
and its chewy, quality card.

XVIII

He bends to pick up the child's book.
Surprised to find it still damp with saliva.
Draped across his palm,

he turns clammy pages and follows
the bright colours of a plausible piper
who is pictured on the streets

of sad little towns, pursued by people,
empty-handed, whose houses are pleading –
doors and windows wide –

"Don't leave us! Don't leave!"
Over the page, he sees crowds blocking
pavements crystal with broken glass,

ragged fiddlers whose bows sweep streams
of music like ticker-tape to burn.
Potters who fire their own hands in the flame

and words unbuttoning from newspapers
and books – all scrapped and sucked into fire.
At the root of flame, a pack of dogs,

each yelping what sounds like "ennui, ennui",
each with the face of the strawberry maid,
the exact same face he had last night.

XIX

He tries to rub this rubbish from his eyes.
Quickly turns pages to destroy the dogs
but fast-forward leaves jagged

stubble fires across the street.
A blue smoke seems to pump up from below.
There's a rainbow overhead,

an odd one, empty.
Embattled beneath, some old-style Wayne-hero
comes from Hollywood, showing his holes.

To his right, at a run, a thin bearded slip
comes slopping a bucket as if for a fire.
To the left, a beauty gone bananas,

her blouse undone, showing gorgeous breasts.
Both running to interfere in something –
he sees it now – their need to find

a redeemable heart – their plea to judges
who don't want to know – and "kyrie, kyrie"
they both call like birds

and wave at him until there's no mistake
(coming out of the blue, it's quite a shock)
the heart they both want to have is his.

XX

He shakes ten pee in spite
from the restoration fund.
At the Mountjoy, wedding guests leave –

the old levered upright and folded
into their sons' unsuitable cars.
A woman with full red lips delves in a bag

for keys, slippery as fish.
She turns her head away, eyes closed
the better to find them and his mother

would do that, hand in her bag
for a purse or something
while the baker stood blocking the door.

As he watches, he sees it's not worth
the wait. He packs the Cavalier
and drives south, more than fast enough

to kill himself if he once lost control.
But don't be concerned.
He's skilled at the wheel. Soon London

closes on him before its lights are lit.
The plane goes east. See! There's London.
David. Don't look so worried. We're safe!

Part Two

Timewise

The digits have flapped
like an animated cartoon book
telling a likely story.

I'm late home because
I've been watching another woman,
knowing she watched me.

I'm the hotter for you.
As I slide into your lap, you laugh
in my face, teeth and tongue

glistening in your mouth,
and grasp me by the wrists.
But a stray finger dabs twice

at a button on my watch.
As we lock our mouths, I hear
the precise *weep weep*.

Teacher

The difference
between the man's body that he has
and the woman's she is beginning to inhabit
is the years between them,
the chain-drag as he walks behind her
and she walks away with friends.

He imagines her body as flawless,
gleaming beneath her dufflecoat,
spirit through the temple wall of flesh.
It sways as she runs to her lesson
in a series of graceful oppositions
like a snake.

Through a glass door he sees her in Maths.
Her scuffed briefcase on a chair beside her.
She is calculating how long it takes
one man to build what others will pull down.

*

His breath grows short with surprise:
the sight of her right hand
 — its half a dozen warts —
as she points to the end of term.

They are standing together at the noticeboard.
He leans (what even he considers to be) too close.
His left arm twitches like a reflex,
wants to fill itself with her, lift
onto her shoulders, into her wiry hair.

Minutes ago, she looked at him,
black eyes wider than was really necessary.

Yet even standing beside her like this,
he's still unable to say:
I can change the dull chalk of myself.

*

They joke and joke
but the energy is unmistakable.

It's the last time he'll see her
and as she sweeps out the door
her laughing advice:
Plenty of fornication!

He remembers the morning
he explained what that word meant.
Remembers the anger when she dodged his class.
Remembers one tired Friday afternoon,
fumbling out her name
instead of Antony's Cleopatra.

Remembers
each morning beside his breathing wife,
when – even then – he dared not own
that hot, unpatrolled dormitory of himself
where she did nothing but sleep and please him.

The Chime Wheel

1. Caen

It's sunrise in our rear-view mirror.
You drive fast, excited as I call

our next destination
in deliberate phoney French –

all the silent letters coming crassly alive –
so you don't misunderstand.

Lacquered headlights blaze back
white municipal signs naming each town.

On the leaving side, they're cancelled
as firmly by other signs

slashed with diagonal red.
Schooled into an English past,

this seems so Gallic:
every town is a brilliant royalty

toppled in a moment. The slash says
the basic value is simply to exist:

the Sartrean teacher's red pen through bad faith.

2. Boulogne

My break-out from family trips
filled with sand, picnics and shrieking rides.
I took my thumb for transport, shelter
a leaky tent and on the last day
I met a dentist from the Ile de France.
His young wife struck unresponsive
with their new child, I imagine
he found it lonely in their holiday villa
— three sugar cubes dropped
on the green, green hills.

We paced the beach: me, in leather sandals,
he, in sensible shoes, dull toe-caps
swinging across the wet sand.
The moon rose with its back towards us.

His wife fed us salad and transparent ham.
Our tongues loosened by white wine,
till I had to pee. The lavatory outside
was a shack — just enough light creeping
beneath the door where it stood at half-mast,
inches above the floor.
Sandals scuffed grit from the beach
as I settled, drunk, on the cold pan
and balanced my head in a V of hands.

I never heard the footsteps.
Just an intake of breath at the bolted door.
A knocking so gentle it should have been
my heart — then, unmistakable,
blocking the light beneath the door,
pushed a round dull toe-cap, moving left and right
like a blinded snout. A thin, pained *please*.
I clung to the seat
in a churning fairground I'd not bargained for.

3. Paris

This was Bohemia at last: couscous
and brandy in a boxroom apartment
at the top of a hundred winding stairs.

No place on the floor for us to sleep.
So we spent the night a few blocks away,
in a separate room Laszlo had to rent.

It was a condition of residence
for a stateless Hungarian student
in France. His subject was language.

He liked to demonstrate how it obscured,
how signifiers slid off the signified,
how the real was a mesh of words.

My grasp was less firm in the morning.
I wanted to fuck you in the shower.
You were too heavy, my arms too weak,

the tiled walls, in torrent, too slippery.
We tumbled out like dogs on heat,
leapt at the release of breaking rules,

chasing Laszlo and his girl, vaulting
the new Metro ticket controls.
A year on, he wakes to her dead beside him,

gassed by a faulty valve in that room.
He's never released her. I hear him still
float her memory in the present tense.

4. Cancale

She smelt of salt.
Her hair, her hands, her dungarees.
The sea was in her and by moving close
I could rouse it for a while.
Then I grazed on a new oyster –
the sweetest, warmest-oiled –
she gladly abandoned to me.
She came, mouthing *yes-yes*
in a Parisian tongue, flat-vowelled,
almost sighing *wet-wet*.

By day, she sold the real thing
from buckets on the quay,
gnarled shells like pebbles in her scoop.
Seventeen francs a kilo.
I have a picture – someone's Citroen jammed
close beside stacked lobster pots,
a trestle table sagging with the tide's weight
of shellfish – there she stands,
proprietorial, right hand on hip,
daring the camera.

Betrayed by the cursive hand
she has stroked over each price tag.
There's a softness in the way the *l*
in *moules* is looped at the top.
I feel her tongue around me.

5. Valras-Plage

I knock at her door.
Within days of catching eye
across a smoke-blue staff-room,
she's on my friend's tarot:
une belle étrangère blonde.
We have stories to tell:
the fourth year horrors,
who treat the *assistante*
to a little English rebellion.

We talk about Woody Allen,
the poems of Thom Gunn,
some shared acquaintance.
Enough to buy drinks
after the school bell.
She had barely any breasts.
A photo of her with *maman*,
rich and topless by a pool.
Two months, gone, saying,
come to Valras-Plage,
I spend my summers there.

I knock at her door – take
her at her word, by surprise.
It's not the beach-house
I imagined. An ugly block
of compartments. Small views
of the Mediterranean.
A mess of washing, towels,
books as she lets me in.
A man in the shower.

On the beach, for an hour,
while he swims, I whisper
clumsily, cruelly to revive
the past. I speak of England
but can't find the words,
out of English or French,
to say how she deceived me,
how her mind's not there,
not attending the moment
till his sleek seal's head
turns back to the beach,
to where she sits alone.

6. Beg Meil

We'd pitched in an old orchard site.
Your face, framed by still school-girl hair,
lifts from a steaming pan beside the tent.

I'm skinny, sheepish on a deserted beach,
before we pull out the baguette and jam for lunch,
before half a dozen wasps panic you so,

we charge off
and leave all the money we have in the sand.
A shot of me at the bank Crédit Agricole,

waiting a telex from your father
to bail us out of a mess. It's for all this
ten year old stuff, we come back again.

Changed, of course. The blackberries
in the hedges were ripe – not now.
So many of the old apple trees are dying –

only balls of mistletoe in their branched heads.
Doves still drone "We love love, do you?"
"We love love, do you?"

And we are better off now.
If we lost everything again we would pay
by Visa. We have a place of our own,

a reliable car, a better stereo . . .
And though we better understand ourselves,
your storms, my freezes, our long

equality, our own islandedness,
the shared lack of sociability that makes
one good company for the other,

we still bicker on holiday.
Over-consideration amounts to indecision,
a clotting-up of energy

into murmurings misheard . . .
There are new gravel tracks at Beg Meil.
We prefer things as memory has them.

Tourists have arrived – the beach where
our francs and travellers cheques sank into sand,
is noisy, smells of cooking and sun oil.

We stay a while, then slip away
by ourselves. Without needing to check,
we carry everything with us.

7. Confort

Two tourists stopping to hear the chime wheel,
we pull off the road at the church of Confort.
For centuries its ring of bells has sounded.

The tongue of a mute-born child began to move
and her parents set up this worm-eaten wheel,
their mark of gratitude for a miracle.

These days it's turned by a tug on a rope.
It has the power to give speech to the dumb.
I pull it for a quickening of my own tongue.

But after all this, what is there left to say?
Each a twist of gristle and conscience.
Part-past, part-now, anxious for what's to come.

Before the wheel's lost the energy I gave it,
a fat German boy squeals and yanks on the rope:
There is terror behind the hands' revolve –

it's the clock face you will not live to see.
Bells sound and ease, cantering quickly to
silence: *Your love will not outlive the day.*

Think – man, woman, mute child – how they loved.
But the thing itself died with them . . .
The sun is cooling. We leave people taking turns

to pull the rope. I come away clutching straws:
Lovers, while they move, hardly feel the hour.
The bells chime only when we lend them power.

Evening creeps like a blue fog at the edge
of our rear-view mirror. A mile of silence.
At the lights, I take your hands from the wheel,
kiss you as I can in the moments before green.

Afterwards

I tread the darkened hall to the bathroom.
The warm morning air is sweet-saturated

with the apple-oil you love to bathe in.
Damp footprints like kidneys cross the floor.

On the dimpled white flat of the bath,
your black hairs are an experiment with the alphabet:

every letter unhinged in the struggle to say
what our bodies found easy as breathing.

I'm sated as the towels hanging heavy with water.
Limpid as the fresh I run from the tap.

Viewing a Room

Where blue-blown roses are printed
across the purple ground of each bedspread
and green-blue leaves are prostrate between.
Where two divans support rolls of bedding
stiff as sleeping figures.

Where curtains fence out the light,
behind a vegetation of bruised plum and grass.
Where the carpets are the colour of slate.
Where the sole relief rises
stalked and too tall between the beds —
white and glossy, a puritan lamp.

Its dusty bulb, a clouded, weary eye,
urging part-plea, part-prohibition:
don't stop here, don't stay in the blue-rose room.

Seeing Stephen

At the end of the first week of Wimbledon,
a spoiling cloudburst swills the windscreen
as I turn through the hospital gates.

In the lift, nurses are in their element,
gossiping across towels and pill trolleys,
danger-red bags of infected linen.

He's in a separate room for my visit.
The moment I arrive, the faded brown sketch
on his pillow-case blurs. He is shaking

his head: freckles in ginger relief,
nose taped like a sun-block. Transparent tubes
seem to drain him so he hardly disturbs

the horizontal of his covers. I stay, talk
small – his view of cloud scudding somewhere
over tennis courts, the coverage on a bedside

portable. *Is this live?* I say. *Or repeats
from last year?* He stares the length of a crisp
white rally. He wants me to translate

now so much energy is unknown to him.
I leave him sitting with a nurse, guilty-
glad to find again the chatter in the lift,

but we stall at the 5th. The lift itself
is sick for a moment. Eyes meet others –
the bedside visitor's panic to find talk,

questions to fill the growing quiet – till
with a soundless nudge, gentle earthward tug
that any body might suffer as the soul
goes free, the lift sinks to street-level.

From the Fridge

Your red t-shirt hangs empty
at our bedroom window, where
the evening breeze will dry it.

The kitchen door is wedged open.
The sound of you busy with a grater
reaches me out on the lawn,

lying still with paper and pen,
rendering down the things we do.
You rattle a plastic cold-box.

The fridge door clamps shut.
I decide to make a poem for you,
to write that box (though it's cold

and damp from the fridge) so it sheds
its milky and uninspired self
and reminds you of me. Full

of the functional, business-
like and unlovely, your hands
on pan handle and kitchen knife,

start back, surprised, as if burned
as you brush against the cold-box:
my cool arm in bed, a stirring

under your hand, the smooth white
of shoulders as they grow warm . . .
You step to the doorway, flick

a light-switch. You glance out.
I miss catching your eye
to check the truth of all this.

But it is true. Your red t-shirt
twists on its hanger,
a sympathetic shiver of pleasure.

Walking Blencathra

The final wet miles
off the mountain-side.
You're hooded, stepping ahead,
resolute vertical

among the flanks of hills.
I break my rhythm —
snagged on thinking
about ordinary days.

I want to apologise.
At thirty-five, perhaps
you thought I'd be cured
of that quiet withdrawing,

the walled-up distraction
after working too long
at the back-room desk.
Coming off Blencathra,

feet find their own way
down narrow sheep-tracks
scored yellow in the grass.
A sense of rhythm,

weather and hillscape
where our bodies know best.
So for hours, we will walk
needing hardly a word

to point a slant of light,
or where a beck divides.
You don't misunderstand,
say *what are you thinking?*

since we both love to walk,
even love each other more
at the foot of the hill,
after such full silence.

Listen. I will explain —
those hurt evenings, hours
when my thoughts draw
on this different rhythm,

when I walk into
my heart's rough weather,
you stand up where the beck
divides, ahead, unhooded.

Visiting the Columbarium

Because there's no letter from her again today,
he invites them deeper into the Castle's root.
It takes a key the size of a tablespoon,
a watery torch no better than a candle,
a sawn-off curtain-rail to tap their way in
like the blind.
                        They pass from the realm
of live water, the click and trill of birdsong,
the humidity of grass, deliberation of bees,
to the bare chutes and cisterns that lie below:
red sandstone hollowed with the ease of clay.
The peck marks of dark-loving, introverted
birds crowd every surface where ancient picks
have worried channels in this rosy cliff.

At the farthest end, the columbarium
is a cave lined with sculpted nesting boxes.
It's a mail sorting office fallen out of use,
a necropolis, its system of orderly files
for ashes in tiny urns. And there is loose ash
in every compartment, cold and dusty
between finger and thumb. "Hundreds of doves –
reared here in the old days for meat in winter –
an endless supply that reproduced itself."

After eating and whisky and drowsing sleep,
he goes back down there, this time barefoot.
A penance: he knows he should ring her and speak.
He taps down the passage. The torch still sheds
no more light than a candle. He hears sounds –
a fluid, glottal sighing, a rustle and scratch –
as he turns the corner and has one second to see
the city of doves, its populous, untidy mind.
Every dark crevice sheltering its sprung head,
a beak moaning with love, black teardrop eyes
in which he glimpses, reflected, a forked

creature, tiny, brandishing a fading light.
The eggs are warm in the depths of each nest.
The heads of young are eager white fingers
that will all be fed.
                One second to see this –
then the cave's a tearing froth as its thousand-
layered petticoat flings past him, to a crack
of light, till his bared head, neck and arms
disappear in blood-hot feathers, the tiny rasps
of beak and claw. Stick, torch and key twist
from his grip. He's sucked into the slipstream
of panicking doves as they vent like a cloud
of white sighing steam from cracks in the cliff.

Above the wooded moonlit gorge, his shaking arms
find balance. Chest puffed and thickened by ropes
of new muscle to row through air. Toes shrivelled
and tucked, neck fluid and sprung and his lips –
a sting of pain, trace of blood – grow glossy
sharpened horn and know nothing of reticence,
restraint – become bubbling celebrants of love.
With a twist of wing, he has the angle of home.

Part Three

Glassmaker

With a long pole,
his sweating assistant scoops a knob
of glass from the glowing cauldron,
looks for a sign — a grunt, a nod —

slips the cue to his master
who guides it towards a thorny stalk
where he snips off a fragment
to work with.

The glass grows crisp as it cools,
begins to ring beneath his touch.
He is building a rose,
watched by a crowd who dawdle

between the hotel and St Mark's.
They're no more than a knot
of silhouettes at the workshop door.
Behind them, brutal sunlight

stands upright in the square,
splays white fire round their shoulders.
The pole sweeps, relentless,
the hand of an old-fashioned clock.

Each squeeze of glass
marks the pink-bright birth
of a new petal, each flawless
and unnatural, until the last

which takes the craftsman's touch,
a hint of being overblown,
a deft turning-back.
But the watching group has sagged

and gapped, the siren call
of lunch, wine, a long afternoon.
He secures the whole frail labour
to one laden rod

which he heaves up, and over,
plunges it suddenly like a foil
into the scorching heart of the kiln.
Stragglers drift away —

the numbing of chill wine in a glass
already on their fingers.
Behind them, the rose brightens
where it ought to be ash.

Lame Ali

after Yashar Kemal

If it is not today
then it will be tomorrow
for sure, as sure
as anything could be.
When he's in pursuit,
head pushed forward,
nothing remains
as it's always been
because his eyes
make little sense
of this wide world.
He forgets everything
and cannot tell
the bad from good.
It's his kind of madness.
And if not today
then tomorrow for sure,
because he must follow
the snapped twig,
the scuffed turf,
the broken blade,
the directions of ash.
Following directly
across the reedbed
where he grows anxious,
catching sight
of a jackal print
which he cannot pass.
It draws him away
deeper into the swamp
where he will revel
in his skills
and revile himself
until he has dragged
his lame foot far

back to dry land.
Then, admiringly,
This is a wise jackal,
Lame Ali says. *My eyes*
at work might forget
the wide world
but sure as anything,
if it is not today
then tomorrow for sure,
I will track him down,
this sly one who walks
with his weight
so thrown forward.
Certainly tomorrow
for sure, as sure
as if I'd placed him
there myself.

Moths

On the aisle marked Soap and Toiletries,
she was brushing at her lapels. Then she bent
and swept at her knees with the back of her hand.
I'd heard the rumours – how she was always busy
about the house, making, re-making beds
to chase caterpillars from between the sheets.

She mentioned her son. I'd known him at school.
He used to follow me round – I'd cut him dead
and never once wondered whether his mother knew.
A hand suddenly flapped at the surrounding air.
"He'll marry soon," she said, "I'm sure you will too?
Though to tell you the truth, I'm not really so well.
You see the problem? Such wonderful creatures,
but moths, all the time, they do pester so,
they pitch and tickle till it drives me mad . . ."
Then she moved to the tills, using a magazine
to flick at her breast, some troublesome spot.

Out of touch for months and the rumour's changed.
They say that she's dead, but I saw her today,
under the milky-bland strips of the supermarket,
by the razors and shampoo, hand deep in her purse
for change. She looked up. She saw me and snapped
the clasp and the air was alive with feathery
antennae. It grew hazy with dust from a thousand
wings that thickened above us, pitched upon her
and rested, slowly rippling like heat that folds
above a flame. There was change in my pocket.
So I pressed two coins softly onto her eyes
and she was gone – silver dropping from my thumb.

Music School

He played pitch-dark piano for silent films.
Next day wrapped a tie around his neck
to conduct the choir through oratorios.
On Sunday the organ sang in Seaham chapel
to ease every soul out of six working days.
The blood of his family thick with music.
In those days, he and his young brother, Sam,
like Sunderland's slick wing and centre half,
had that much instinct, fiddle and ivory
drew the stamp of working men's boots –
didn't know themselves where the next twist
would lead. Still hit the refrain together.

Come dawn, back down their hole in the ground,
there was moleskin, snap, slapping, hollering.
He and Sam, they dreamed a school of sound
to teach kids like them to coax music out
before any soot-cough could brick it in.
But you need spirit to venture such
and the war had ripped his at the root,
though he saw no action – his twisted legs,
where props came down, saw him clear of that.
Later, years spent playing for richer men
in floating palaces between Liverpool,
New York. For them, he made a brittle sound
to match the flutter of bank notes.

Now, white string-works show in his hands.
His skin is marked like foxing on a Bible.
'The Creation' was the last sacred work he played.
He says the darkest times were his best,
when dust motes were fireflies overhead.
The projector beam seemed a wind of light
that never ruffled a hair on anyone's head,
but blew him to gusts of music. Never failed –
but once. Flickering newsreel from the Front.

He sat plugging out major patriotic chords,
bent forward in praise of that great light,
when Sam was in it, above him, smiling,
puppet-waving, jerky, shin-deep in mud
where he should have been . . .
Last time he ever saw him in living flesh.
He still hears it. How that last projector
reeled laughter out of the silence he made.

The Fisherman

for Tom Rawling

I cast my mind over the Greta river,
watch a fisherman sign the evening
with a cursive flourish.
He is the image of Alice.

A stalker through riverbank dark,
under a sudden showering of dew.
His feet usurp the ancient right of eyes;
they tell the ground like a braille.

His milky ghost glides through bramble,
whole skin the opened sensor
of more than touch. The night
has grown bigger than his books,

his preparation for this sleekbacked
ale-darkness, the mirror shards of water.
When it's finished, he'll gladly talk,
how he treasures his privilege.

How it is not so much
the pale torpedo he lays neatly
on the riverside, dead, so diminished,
but the stealth to steal a glance

beyond the looking-glass, where
the trembling whorl wobbles and breaks.
Bright-eyed, he says it never shows
the stamp of any world he knows.

One End of Empire

Orange globes burn in the trees at twilight.
I can barely distinguish lanterns from fruit.

In the distance, blue mountains shoulder snow.
A bird will cry. I remember an avalanche

of fifty years ago, how it struck a night
such as this – a mere puff of white – a duster

being flapped clean from an upper window.
A hundred dead. Not a sound on the veranda.

Grain's Gill

He lost his wife out on the fells.
Every weekend, he took a bus there to walk,
to photograph and record his love.
Each weekday evening, he'd lay out weapons —
pen, paper and India ink — and inscribe
every footstep into snow white sheets.

After seven years of this, she upped and left.
And he could hardly begrudge her that.
Though he's lost without a woman to cook,
lay out his winter shirts, he didn't,
in the stony bottom of his heart, much care
because the fells gave him a kingdom
that spread more readily for his pleasure.
He wanted only solitude and to be driven
like lightning to strike
and strike again at the highest points.

As she left, his white sheets were bound
into books. He used the local chippie
as a kind of hearth, but home was the rock
and heather, sheep-cut turf, closer
to heaven than any other plot of earth,
though paths soon grew to rivers of gravel
under the boots of people carrying his books.

Yet there were peaks remote enough
to be conquered in solitude. Till last year,
Grain's Gill, a misty day, slippy on the path.
He's surefooted as a goat, yet slithered
and hobbled into every rut and boulder.
It wasn't the mist, nor the grease of rain,
but the gathered up gloom of years
spent scratching beneath a 40 watt bulb
left him squinting, impotent on the path.

Now he rehearses a single afternoon,
when swifts in dozens dived a summit cairn
made bloody with wind-blown ladybirds.
A double miracle: a helpless banquet
for those knife-edged birds that fell thickly
as arrows and each puff and flick
across the back of his hand was a kiss,
their touch on his cold brow, a crowning.

From The Museum of Mankind

The body's tall upright is a lopped log,
ready-made for an attack of knives.
Rough-cut wood cubes serve as feet
for a figure, whose spindly arms are
weighed with the suggestion of hands —
yet almost obscured
by the raised hackles of so many blades.

The head is skilfully worked:
flattened nose, brows arched over eyes
that open ingenuously in a face
that is apparently without malice.
It seems the knives and nails
have shied clear of too intimate
an attack, until they cluster
instead on either side of the head,
a steely bristling of Victorian whiskers.
Paterfamilias. Ragged god.

His worshippers have made him porcupine
by the stab of old kitchen knives,
the hammering of masonry nails,
the piercing of steel, slow screw of hooks.
This must be a god who loves pain,
one who calls for a last frenzy,
an awesome limbering up for holy war.
This is the idol of those fierce for certainty.
They see no further than the obsidian pebble,
the raw fact of violence under the human heart.
They use only the language of blades.

I was milked to manhood in another devotion.
I prayed to a god, not brother of this log.
I believed my elders ate and drank him.
I remember standing and kneeling in ranks.
I remember singing my heart out
as hands and feet were hammered to a tree.

A Carved Flute

for Nick

At first nothing, rich yolk gristling
into blood, wing and voiceless bill.

A grown speck, warm on the breast-down
of my galleon-mother . . .

The world a mound of shrivelled weed,
an oiled reach of water from which

I cower on her back. Cattle-herded
down the Thames, bill notched for Dyers'

or Vintners' or Crown, I strengthen
with each moult, take to flight, mute-

throated, loud in the throb of air
on feather. I re-build the castle mound

but die choking on some bitter weed.
Where I drift to the reedbed, grow dry

and misshapen, maggots unweave me.
Comes a man who rips a wing-bone out –

hollowed clean, his fingers find stops
and now his breath gives voice to song.

Lark

I hear it punish itself with singing.
The sky it fills is the effort it makes

to see how every landmark lies: threads
that link them run through its head

like smoking rope through an eyelet.
Even when a merlin finds it out,

for a minute four wings in dogfight
shear air, spindling, crest over claw,

all the while gulping breath to sing,
claim its place, say the merlin's part

of that, show strength to be tapped
till the hawk's will gives. The merlin

shrugs its dark self and leaves
the open sky, the lark's song, unbroken.

Tidal

With the tide ebb, the bay sits full
of blackened, carious teeth.
The rocks string gold and green weed.

In a flurry of gull calls, flakes of snow,
the tide returns. The mouth becomes
its blue water. Sun makes it sing with light.

There is filth from every tidal song.
The palate grows a whelming of residue
sucked down to the fruit of the sea.

The Greek Gifts

I

Half a kilo of ham.
One kilo of tomatoes.
A dozen eggs; a bottle of retsina.

'Atheist' in Greek
means simply 'god-forsaken'.

You meet an old friend
on the boat to Samos.
You meet your new colleague's wife
for the first time.

Call a doctor, please.
I require assistance.
Do you speak my language?

Now turn to cassette two.

II

"Don't worry with the language, my boy.
There really is no mystery in Greece.
The modern country – it's a shit-heap.
For the ancients, you must look at the face
of the kouroi – wide-eyed, smiling,
yet not right to call them serene.
There's too much energy in the muscles of the face.
Lips drawn back in the very moment
of a smile. They will never break decorum.
They will never break into a laugh.
Difficult to describe.
Try perfect."

III

On the third night a great wind blew.
In a dream he met his colleague's new lover.

He was woken by a worm
boring his left ear – a hiss in its throat,
its head gauded with gentle pain.
The bed was a desert.

On the Areopagus, voices raised
in pursuit – the furies of modernity
crying, "Could ever such beauty guilty be?"

IV

A picture of a single black olive
and a few narrow leaves.
A golden scrotum of oil hangs
on the dark round, lit from the left.

He insists that the oil of the olive
is the only secret of Greece.
"It's the balanced composition
of consumable fatty acids.
A veritable oil of life."

His face,
tanned by too much tobacco and sun,
nudges my elbow to pour a swathe
across pasta and goat-meat sauce.
"Good for the stomach,
good for the blood and skin,
good for a sexy massage."

Have I heard that the sound
of one hand clapping
is the slap of belly into another's rump,
sliding in the golden oil?

V

Where three roads cross.
Where Oedipus killed his father,
we row over what tape to play.

Corinth. Athens. Thebes.

I want something with a tune.
Even in this place, caught unaware:
the influence of parents.

We fight
over the sweetness of the past
and the rap-fragmented present.

VI

Always the penis, ends of noses.
Often hands lopped back to the elbow.
Bony feet and lower shins,
even those protected with greaves.
These are the bits that are lost.

In the museum,
I need a break from this torrent
of amputees. Yet the worse it gets
the more affecting it becomes.

This man – a tranche of torso
supported in a modern metal frame,
the rock's core open to the air
and above float two sections
of a once-connected head;
a back-right scalping of hair;
an upper front scallop of eye
and glorious cheekbone
and half a noble brow . . .

I recognise him now.
An acquaintance I once met
on the boat to Samos.

VII

A mile of white road.
A trestle table. A grass verge.
The man wears a hat.

Three kilos of silvery fish.
He brings the morning's catch.
He sets them on the table.
Look! What gleaming cutlery!

I have dulled my sense with alcohol.
Call a doctor, please!
Is there anything left to say?

Oh, the orange trees burn all over the Peloponnese!

Now turn to cassette three.

VIII

Like a god
I wear the leather of Nike on my feet.
Yet the caretaker of the Olympian temples
sits on a tumbled slice of fluted column
and sings a descending melody.
It's gypsyish, halfway to a hymn,
some lament for love long ago.

The Greeks
built here from shell-full rock.
Grown pitted with millenia
of rain following sun,
the columns of Zeus' temple
are downed by a tremble of the earth.
Stacks of coin six feet across.

In a ring of hills, rocky, uneven,
the scrub still green in this February,
spirits brood over the demolition.
One of them spits
into the grass between verses.

IX

Who are the kouroi?
Those who don't fart,
whose fleshy creases don't smell as the day wears on,
who never run out of things to say,
who don't blather in embarrassment,
who wouldn't think that wanking's better than sex
because you can please yourself,
who wouldn't forget anniversaries
or be troubled by infidelities
(their partner's, or their own),
who wouldn't yearn,
suffer their own incompleteness,
or dream up gods, or posit eternity,
who wouldn't need to try out new things
to spice a jaded appetite,
who wouldn't learn by their mistakes.
Those who have no need to call a doctor,
those who are not god-forsaken,
those

those

X

Sick of stone-cold nakedness.
Pert nipples you'd crack your teeth on;
the fixed smile of well-developed pectorals;
pebble-bellies of abdominals;
high buttocks swollen to take the down-weight
of marble torsos; the sweet-meats coolly
stowed in their loose sacks;
the well-regulated prick at rest . . .

In the shower, the flesh gives and is warm.
I sense the hollow space in my chest,
soaping beneath my arms. I feel
muscles slide in their oily sheaths,
the weight of the head lifting to take
hot water full in my face. The frizz
of pubic hair no sculptor can translate.
My body has a heat and weight of its own.

When you are ready, turn off the tape.

Part Four

On a Roman Road

for Bruce Barnes

Where I cycle towards a few days respite –
uncertain, off to a writers' retreat –
legions delineated their purpose.

Scored by its cars, the slick black road
sheers off. I pedal ahead, up a lane
that's muddy, rutted, my backwheel heavy

with books and belongings so the front
feels light and airy, out of balance.
But that's fine, now I bump and weave

through the potholes of this Roman way,
this moth-eaten ribbon from Caesar's skirt,
a ragged line of the imperial orders.

Long descent to the cottage of writers.
The fizzy, odd imprecision of steering
is worse at speed as the heavy baggage

about my backwheel powers me on
till I go half where I intend to go,
half following the contour of the ground.

But that's fine. I'm flying, exultant.
I will print my own way, this hand leading,
this being led, to the foot of the hill.

Wasps

I wake from dreams of a schoolmaster
whose insecure shed has been raided –
whole classes of ancient exam scripts
chewed to sculpt a wafery, growling nest.

At lunchtime, my beer is suddenly angry,
fouled by a rattling drowner in hoops.
He spirals like a drunk in the froth.
I help him out. He dries for minutes
in the sun, then flies a perfect S-shape
into a spider web. Within seconds,
bitten, rolled in grey thread,
just his sting-needle showing, moist,
pulsing, again, again . . .

A whole nest is rooted out next door.
The queen is gone, the soldiers dead –
for twenty-four hours workers return
to nothing they recognise and at night
one the size of a cat drifts through
my bedroom window, its hum like thunder.
Jointed twiggy legs hold me down
beneath a swivelling, oiled head
as uncommunicative as stone.
Its long abdomen is like a cob of maize
I find velvety to the touch . . .

Next morning, there in the window,
an inch-long wasp walks in silhouette,
sluggish, disoriented, hobbling its V
of wings back and forth –
less than, more than, less than . . .
There is a waspishness in me this morning.
I will eat my toast with jam.

Shoe Pieces

1. Sandals

Cut from Turkish leather,
nailed and sewn into a Turin shroud
for my hot feet,

I will celebrate my sandals.
Where the satin of sweat darkens
into a Friday shape —

the arch alone, a virgin half-moon
of original hide.
Where detailed indentations

of my ten toes — tarsals,
metatarsals, phalange —
show with the clarity of X-ray.

Where points of special stress
grow black with heat and moisture:
a strap's looped underside;

tide-marks where the buckles clip;
where toes curl and flex
into the left-right-left of a walk

that carries me everywhere.
Be gone, you other footwear!
You toy shoes of childhood

with snowy, spongey soles,
each cut from bright leather
like Absalom's best —

with "Poules window corven on his shoos".
You schoolboy brogues,
all scuffed and trampled,

stuffed with socks in changing rooms.
Brown desert boots in untended
suede that sponge up rain

under sail-like flares.
You trainers with technological soles.
Frayed and flapping espadrilles.

You jellies on vacation.
Smart toe-pinchers for interviews
and weddings – you misery makers!

I say, "Give me my sandals!"
because they sprout with secret wings.
Look, when I turn them over

how can I not love them
for the whorls and weather-systems
on which I walk?

2. Boots

Rounded brown toe-caps
are the wet muzzles . . . of what?
They browse through puddles, mud
and grass. They're at home with thistles,
nettle, thorn – the voice I imagine
is the leathery mooing of contented cattle.
You say, what do they talk about?
"Look around – there is plenty to love!"
And sure enough, every step
has left its token in the caterpillar track
of their soles: grit and dust,
a piece of grass, pale stones like pips
caught in teeth
at the end of a slap-up meal.

Yet they're modest, they bear their scars.
The left has scabs on the toe-cap
where I follow in Doctor Johnson's steps,
refute Berkeley by swinging at rocks . . .
They ride the bald and cobbley pates
of boulders down to Seathwaite Bridge.
I use their snouts to chip out steps
in snow beyond Striding Edge.
And later, stopped in a windswept puddle,
when my head droops and I catch sight
of my solo reflection against the sky:
"Look around – there is plenty to love!"

Loyally they carry me home.
I pamper them with the fat of dubbin.
And these red laces that look out of place,
an added braggadocio of my own,
they serve only to stress the essence
of 'bootness' which is what I like.

Oh, with your padded leather backs,
grip, grip always my ankles high up.
Ride rough-shod under my human soles.

Laugh

The muscles in the throat,
a corded harp till the laugh blows in,
a stiff blast across the shoreline
and a donkey brays.

A sound that carries
further inland than any other.

The muscles relent
and the dull flap of everyday
picks up once more.
The laugh's uninhibition
feels like someone else's folly.

Neighbour

It seemed to me like her sweet revenge.
How she rattled cold ash from the grate
on her side of the semi's shared wall

every snug morning of my childhood.
Her revenge for the night's intrusion –
the way it forced her to be still.

She polished the kitchen waste-pipe
to such a brassy mirror condition
(where its ugly snout drooped from the wall)

that I'd see my face grow long and sour
as I crept past to retrieve a lost ball.
Our windows lolled open all summer:

handkerchief parachutes spun to the ground.
Her windows only swung to be scoured
to the pitch of perfect transparency.

She'd peer out at her husband trimming
their hedge so close it grew miniscule-leaved,
shaped and solid like a cottage loaf.

Our mothers told us and we believed:
at the heart of her kitchen a Raeburn stove's
hot little mouth consumed everything.

We played at that loaf-hedge for years.
Summoned up yells and laughter like a spell.
Never dared ask why she had no children.

The Perfect Companion
(11/2/63)

'I am a nun now, I have never been so pure'

Everywhere winter screws down its white sheet
and Dad clamps me down, getting over-strung
because this is my seventh birthday. *Careful.*

*Sit still. One thing at a time. You'll be tired
before tonight.* Her last night – as it turns out.
So while I make a poor pretence of calm,

she wraps her children like precious eggs
from the cold, drives to the zoo. Always careful.
I chew corners from the jelly concentrate.

Its rubber cubes release their oily-smoke
of flavours under boiling water. Then cooled,
colours burn from glass basins in the fridge.

*

On the frosty flat top of the garden wall,
I watch a thrush lower its tail, squeeze droppings
full of steamy undigested seed.

I unravel them across the crystalline frost
with the stem of a leaf until Dad hauls me in
for playing with filth before lunch –

which she eats voraciously, praising
the roast. Then sleeps till six. The first time
in days she's settled to it. A new resolve.

Getting better. They hope she's getting better.
Chaperoned by tall mothers and fathers,
my friends smudge snow across the threshold.

*

79

She insists on being driven back to the flat,
locked in snow and ice, beside Primrose Hill.
She cries all the way home in the car

as Keith White hands me a pristine Triumph
Herald. She's always loved the whiteness
of bed-linen and with the wrapping in shreds

around my feet, I'm saying it's brilliant,
telling Keith I have one already, battered
and scratched, the perfect companion . . .

*

I tug the stiff handle where the remains
of lemonade have arched to the lavatory bowl,
but Dad collars me on the landing, boils:

*You're rude! You're ungrateful! To say you
have one already! You don't tell the truth!
What must Keith think of us? Go. Say sorry!*

She always loved the white of bed-linen.
She leaves out milk and bread for the children.
This is not usual. She wants to settle her

debt with the Professor whose flat is below
and although I'm in bed for hours, I sleep
only when he hears her pacing the kitchen above.

*

Now the children's eyes close as she tapes
and towels any ventilation. Seals herself in from
discordancy. Folds a neat cloth so her head

need not rest on the cold of the unclean oven.
She crouches down. All the gas taps on.
And the children sail through their sleep,

windows wide on to frosting Primrose Hill
and they dream, as I do, of Keith White's face
in the snow track, crying, abandoned,

miserable and protesting, not one of us has
any need to atone, although Dad still tugs
at my pillow. *Sorry. Say sorry. Apologise.*

Accident

She leaves him, Johnson-powdered,
a dusty nude, squatting on her bed,
a little Buddha, pulling his toes.

The bathroom's a fug where she kept
the gas-heater blasting because he
played for ages in inches of water.

Not vain (just the mirror's well-placed),
she takes a look at herself in passing,
registers something remote and greyed

crossing beneath the condensation.
She pulls out the plug as a ripping
scream panics her back, expecting

bright blood, a disfiguring dive
to the floor, twisted limbs at least.
He still sits plumb on the bed,

reading his palms and wailing a high
continuous wound in the air
at his chubby fingers, their wrinkling.

Grandma's House

So I might never be disappointed,
wanting something to play with
that she couldn't provide,
my grandma collected everything.

Some thought that her collection
was so complete it was another world.
Others saw in the way it summed all things
a possible image of God.

It didn't seem so important to me,
since whenever I asked
for something to play with –
a particular shell, an old model Spitfire,

marbles made of pearl, a beech tree in autumn –
she could never find them
although she swore they were safely stowed
if I would just be patient.

Some First Steps

Gravel bit like scissors into my knee.
Flesh opened with a pouting lower lip,
bled quickly at the rim, white at the root.

She planted me high on a stool at the sink
and bathed the wound, bending low
to pick tiny stones like shrapnel from it.
It hurt like cheese-wire noosed round
trembling bone. So I locked my gaze
to the lowered crown of her mousey head,
to the thick hair's shell-like spiral.

But as the pain began to uncoil,
as she murmured *my little wounded man*,
as she massaged my leg till it burned,
my gaze slipped to where her dress fell loose,
down the receding, egg-freckled, trembling gorge.

Trophies

We stood around the big cartons she brought
home at weekends. We helped unpack
the dry white flowers of tissue paper
that coddled the successes of strangers.

She worked all week for Mr Colbourne.
His men engraved bracelets and pendants.
She sat with his women in artificial light
to proof-read the love, devotion of others.

On Fridays, at the handing out of overtime
to take home, there were only ever pieces
from the bottom of the range — trophies
for Sprinting, Flower Arrangement, Bridge.

She carefully unwrapped cheap rectangles
— gold, silver, and bronze — each one
already engraved. Her job was to peel
their sticky backs and apply them neatly

to a tinny plate cup or mounted medallion.
But first she had to check them for truth.
Rejects got listed for their bogus awards:
100 Yard Splint, arranging *Fowlers*, *Budge*.

I liked to help, especially those trophies
they engraved onto shiny, black, bakelite
and topped with a man standing on one leg,
or a woman waving a stringless racquet.

I always added the finishing touch, rubbing
a white stick of wax into the letters
till they burst from the black to announce
someone's name. Never mine. Never hers.

There were no prizes for being a cog
in Colbourne's works. Gradually part-time;
finally redundancy. Ten years on, at her
first attempt, seven first prizes for jam,

embroidery, cakes and cardigans. We stand
round her prize-work as if it warms our hands,
as if her weeding of error has finally
turned trumps. The white wax blazons her name.

Autumn Leaves

after Millais

Stalled on the leafy hard-shoulder,
his grey retreating hairline dipped
beneath the car's propped bonnet,
he peers hopelessly inexpert
into its oily-warm unworking depth.
His four impatient daughters
stand an untidy line at his side.

They appeal to the passing traffic
with such closed and silent mouths.
The tallest is dark-haired Sophie.
An empty satchel hangs on Alice's arm.
Tilda has already turned half aside.
And dead-eyed Bella seems not to see
the white-scarred apple in her hand.

Gillespie Park

It feels like thunder. But that's not why
the old man is a diver preparing to tip
backwards into another element.

Old – but sprightly, the way he pulls
the sleeve of leggings on like waders.
A thick jacket, crusty with tweed,

too hot for this weather. Then gloves.
It's an arming of sorts as he lowers
protective glasses, held by elastic

like those Dad used to wear every day –
ugly, frog-eyed, on the lathe at work.
Like a hawker without stock, he strings

round his neck a strong Tupperware box.
I break out a few pleasantries
to delay the old man – how long the summer

lasted this year. I don't want to see
him go where he's headed. We fall silent
as I always do with old men alone.

Now he looks about him – the diver again
checking the swell, sky, the horizon,
then backs into the brambles behind me.

He fills his slung box with fat black
fruit, follows the falling contours until
he's up to his neck, hands red with stain

no likely downpour will wash away.
Deeper still. Now one or two bramble-arms
wave over the spot where he's gone down.

My Moonraker Father

It scandalised the domino school.
The family as well. Like most of you
we'd come to think we owned our father.
For himself, he was angry at having won
nothing more than a pint of bitter.
For the price of that, his rutted face
was there for all to see:
in his banded felt hat, flies in the brim,
his mutton-chop whiskers,
collarless shirt, his birthday waistcoat,
right hand raising that innocent, shamming pint.

I was only eight. I couldn't understand.
Some pimply paparazzo took my father away.
The domino school demanded legal action,
so Dad rang the company (that was a time
when he knew how to handle telephones).
They said no deal, explained they'd bought
the copyright on him for the usual fee,
how the photographer had settled up
with the subject before any shutter blinked.
A pint! For his soul? For his stiffened face
to be sold as public property on every
postcard stand in the south and west . . .

And mine too, maybe.
Without meaning to, when I remember
how Dad was tricked to play the yokel fool,
dung-brained cider-swill, whose only dreams
are furrows straight as his pyjama stripes,
ambitions as meagre as the piddling Biss,
and vowels broader than Salisbury Plain,
I feel angry, incapable — must I be son and heir
to that evening the bastard film fixed dead?

Ere's greetins vrum Wilsher in the west,
vull uv isterry an claims tu vaim.
Loik Jaak ere, wi is point a best.
Ee'll tell ee a tale vert glass a zaim —
ow ee maid a vawchewn wun zummer noight,
saw a gert silver crowun in a laik —
(twuz but the moowun but Jaak wuz toight!).
Ee rekked it owt wiv is gert felt at
an zold it negs day vert vivity quid!
Verra point a best, ol Jaak, ee zings
iz story — then ee tells ow iz eldist kid
caatches raindraps ver doimind rings.

There are kicks and kicks.
Dad fell fast under a shower of cards.
Each post sapped him, seemed to erase
something of what he'd been. He put away books,
grew his whiskers out, began to pretend
he couldn't subtract at darts. He took
to smoking a church-warden, grew quiet
and disinclined, refused to take notice
of the national news. He took to barley wine.
But it wasn't the drink that made him
forget himself and withdraw from us —
he was fading out like a television effect,
someone else was fading up in his place.

It's taken years. He must feel lonely.
He barely knows us or himself these days —
answers only to "old Jaak". We've stood by him.
I still do, though it's likely I'll end
my days like him. Late at night, when I look
at rain slanting through a window-light
someone's left on, raindrops glitter
with the crisp white of diamonds . . .
I lean out to see where they hit the grass.
I swear they bounce and roll like stones.

And it may not stop there — but who would
believe me? — I've seen my younger brother
stand by west-facing windows as the sun
is setting and I swear he scrapes the glass
with his pocket-knife, cups his other hand
as if he caught shavings of gilt, or gold leaf.

Part Five

A Long-House in the Forest

I

His war happened in the blazing Middle East.
When he was young, far from the mud of Europe
and the wired camps, his thighs were burned
by too much bravado, sitting astride
the exhausts of a Hurricane that hadn't cooled.
He picked up the language. Never liked Arabs.
Any dark skin's still a nigger to this day.
So he votes for the Right, though he's careless
of politics and takes it as read: we all
long for power and we all need to be led.

II

In his dream, he is Caspar. He has chosen
to wait in the draughty long-house, watching
the yard collect its ragged slush of leaves.
He knows the corn-bins are flooded and rotten.
He knows this month is the anniversary
of nights when Caspar rolled in distress, youth,
dream illumination – an excited showing
of power's open hearth, its air-gulping fire –
his sleep filled with the birth of a king
whose strong arm would invigorate the world.
At once, Caspar instructed a journey. His gift
for this new king, of course, was gold.

III

A wretched child asleep on that year's straw.
Neither mother nor father people of consequence,
but simple Jews – trouble-making, deluded.
This was nothing worth his understanding.
(He knows Caspar is a man of wisdom and books.)
What could be the need for this powerless figure?

Why this pot-bellied brat? This futile gesture?
Shepherds stood with doting faces for the boy.
He turned his back, dropped the derisory gift.

IV

Without wishing, Caspar gleaned what became
of the lad from travellers' unlikely tales.
How he saw no reason to cloak humility.
Nor saw the need to make a show of strength.
No surprise the authorities destroyed him.
And on that day, Caspar, his dream-self,
was driven by dreams again, north this time,
to the Black Sea, fighting the Danube inland,
to this blond-haired, beer-drunk, long-limbed place,
whose people mistake him for a piece of Hell
with his blackened face and barbarian tongue.

V

Sitting by the squadron's crest, a photograph
of the kids, he sees no reason to dream himself
black and ignorant, plagued by dreams. But he is
Caspar, has chosen the long-house and struggles
at night – not with dreams of the hot south,
of home, courtyards, frescoes and fountains –
but with a dream that has no place yet, though
he searches for it, now that same, futile boy
in the straw has grown his only dream-guide
and weeps over this precise, god-forsaken ground.
He finds it ruled by those whose failure is to see
no need for an icon of the weak, the needful.
Here, the boy's deluded people prove no trouble at all,
filing from wooden huts ranged like inland galleys,
to incinerators smoking in the German forest.

On Whistler Mountain
(New Year 1991 – New Year 1993)

in memory of Richard Burns

"I am the enemy you killed, my friend.
I knew you in this dark"

I

I'm weeping on the phone. It's a wipe-out.
The satellite's long delay leaves her words
hanging between continents: Europe
breathless to receive; North America
anxious for some response. Each putting trust
in contact suspended only, not broken-down.

II

The phone back in its cradle. My mind
blanks out, but for one insistent human
figure, squat and huddled, eyes wide
with terror – Chris, you must remember him –
fingers long and weak and incompetent.
A knot-hole like a sudden gunshot in his chest.

I know where he sits. An afternoon two
years ago, when four of us were gazing
(not Andrew who had scuttled away,
found later frightened of the masks),
four gaping drop-jawed at a totem-pole,
under its spotlights and careful humidity.

It seemed, from one rough foot to its topmost
point, a rocket-blast of animation
and caricature. A weird narrative –
sense and pleasure from sequence – that set me
talking, typical, assured, how language
was invented out of our hunger for stories.

III

Now I have one. New Year. The west coast.
I'd backed off the world for pleasure,
a little local colour – the totem
amongst pelts and pots, canoes, doorposts
carved with beasts and heroes, squat images
of gods, implements of war, whose descendants

had been gathering for the last five months
on the hot sand of the world's other side.
That bright young city had stalled under
a knee-deep snowfall, shed its usual
gridlock of guzzlers on Robsonstrasse –
for days, a motorless park with scarved-up walkers.

Air-conditioning vents, strained and moaning
in each alley, their out-breath the only
melt to be seen. All flights cancelled. Lucky,
we thought. Chris had met us hours before
the big fall: we seemed chosen, pampered guests
in an exclusive club the size of the city.

IV

I dab the ansaphone on. Impossible
to run the risk of more tears from more talk.
To lend such bad news breath is surely to screw
the knife . . . I wipe the TV mid-
phrase on exclusion zones to north and south,
eighteen months after we thought the war was over.

V

I'd never have believed the way we'd come
apart, all but lost what I'd trusted in:
our common blood, brothers' understanding.
Once, kids at a loose end, we both wandered
into waste ground behind the village church –
a brambled mason's yard from an earlier age.

I've always clung to what we found there . . .
I loved words – almost a sufficient world.
He loved what they labelled, saw molecules,
atoms, moved from physics to maths. His quick
fingers grew hungry for the garbled keys
of computers. So he rode them, meteoric,

across the Atlantic, to a silicon
Klondike. *Come skiing. Just get yourselves here
and we'll pay.* So we gaze at the totem,
its Haida craftsmen from Queen Charlotte
all but wiped out by the white-man's smallpox
before this century had steadied on its feet.

VI

I remember it. A hollowed, rough-hewn
canoe, its red-cedar wood bird-pecked
and chiselled into a naive story
that said: BlackBird – who created the world –
hops and flaps around the place he's just made,
quite post-coital after his creative chore.

He can't, of course, stretch for his Lucky Strikes –
this is the mythic past – but he's hungry.
So he flies up to the cliff-edge at Naikoon,
sees killer whales in their natural place,
great jaws spilling with so many sweet fish.
People from a nearby village, walking the beach.

Like whales they eat only fish from the sea.
BlackBird is envious. It's unfair:
his belly aches while these less-deserving
feed so well. His stomach grumbles, *Do it now*.
He glides down and darkens the village roof.
I ask: "What did she say before I came to the phone?"

VII

New Year's eve. On the corner of Granville
and Georgia, the five of us, snug on seats
by the window, pack away hot pizza.
My gaze gets snagged by the Hong Kong Bank,
where a dull brassy gleam winks our way
as if it's counting change, or maybe counting down.

The New Year begins. Hugging optimists.
Balloons untethered and the band plays on.
I kiss my girlfriend and my brother's wife.
Then my brother. We dance around Andrew,
arms-on-shoulders, turn to applaud guests
in the expensive hotels that line City Square.

They drop party streamers: white toilet rolls
unravelling on the face of the building.
And in the Hong Kong Bank, the gleam swings on.
At precisely the same slow interval.
A pendulum. Twenty-six metres long.
Swaying above the customers' heads like a sword.

VIII

"You want to know what she said before I
called you to the phone? Go and get Martyn.
Tell him to sit down. I knew what it was.
She didn't have to say another word.
Remember? The last time we saw them was
the airport, the night the Gulf war deadline ran down.

Crazy. She says she blames herself. She says,
I have no idea what I'm guilty of.
But I can't stand up, say I'm innocent!"
BlackBird all but gags on what he can see.
The tasty fish-shoals are so plentiful.
The people of the village are so content.

The men set lines at dawn, haul each one,
quivering, to the women's cooking fires.
The more he sees, the less BlackBird sees
each individual woman and man.
He hides as the silver catch comes to shore,
then wipes out men with a sudden whack of his bill.

Women wail and mob. He sweeps up the fish
into the black cloak of his wing.
I was first to see it in the rubble.
We'd mucked in the mason's yard for a while,
putting stones through ruined sheds' black eyes
from a ball-pitcher's plate of raised grass and rubbish.

I remember, as I twisted for power
(I never had the strength of Chris's arm),
how my heel caught against something solid.
In the grass, clean lines of something stood out,
shaped but abandoned, a defective thing
— so Chris assumed — but I wanted to dig it out.

IX

What we turned up that day is still here
by the fire, where Louise gapes at the flame.
Firelight warms stone till I can almost see
its wings twitch. "Remember? At the airport?
Chris couldn't wait, with Andrew already
climbing baggage conveyors. The airlines expecting

hijacks, bombs, on the midnight deadline.
So even then it had begun to go wrong.
We were travelling. Yet we waved them off."
As they left, Chris said nothing but *Goodbye*.
The boards reddened with delays . . .
For the first time in weeks, we talked about the war.

X

I try on the technology. Slip clips
to open each boot's plastic orange-beak
and slide my foot into its padded cell.
I must be mad. Chris, why didn't we talk?
The clips again and the boots' wires tighten
to press me forward as if fighting a strong wind.

What Chris does say is, "Lean out of the slope!
Plant the pole downhill. Follow the damn thing!
Don't be frightened. Finish the turn and then
plant again. Punch with your fist! Practise
attack – lean out – plant down – punch out –"
I see myself crashing, tail-up ostrich in snow!

XI

BlackBird gobbles the dead villagers' haul.
On the totem-pole, a squat fisherman
in a tall hat, mouth cut to half a snarl,
jealously clutches the tails of two fish,
athletic, arching across his broad chest.
His toes clamp the head of a figure below:

a shag-pile shaman that looks like a bear.
He instructs the fishermen to get revenge.
We raise no complaint – we each have our reasons –
as little Andrew wipes out the build-up
in the sand to play a video-game:
a schematic green frog crossing a busy road.

"There! Like father, like son," his mother says,
as he rattles the joystick and frog skips
clear. Cars plough into each other instead.
"Child's play," grins Chris. And for the umpteenth time
I ask him what it is he really does.
"It's this sort of thing. But more so. Serious games.

Glorified calculators, if the truth
be told – which I can't, of course. Some neat maths
and clever applications. It's a breeze.
Surgical stuff. You'll see. You still keep
that old stone fossil we found? Like that.
It sniffs whatever you want from the rubbish heap."

XII

Briefly in the air over Puget Sound,
we sank towards Seattle, the Seahawks
Kingdom in the sunset, a red button
on the dark criss-cross shirt of the city.
Our drop-in delayed. We don't disembark.
Each piece of baggage off-loaded, checked again.

XIII

We can't both stare at this fire all night . . .
I drink whisky. It sharpens my headache.
We've hardly spoken – all possible words
are fraught with the way things used to be, so
quite useless now, except to recite facts:
"He must have been dead by about this time last night."

But he still plays out his life the moment
I lie down (side by side, but contact too
has lost its mute, sweet eloquence for us).
He's still there on the slope. Waiting. Making
a fluent dash for the farthest snow brim,
he kicks a feathery white fan. Again, waiting . . .

XIV

Time ran out as we crossed the Hudson Bay.
The fishermen did as the shaman said.
They changed their hooks and set the lines once more.
The halibut swarmed in those fertile times.

The catch came silver and heavy to the shore.
Already gorged, BlackBird swooped to the feast

and with every fat fish he snatched away,
his head grew heavy as the hooks went home.
The fishermen hauled in a tug-of-war –
BlackBird's lightning smash and grab immune
no more. Sick and panicking, he's slowly
reeled in. The fish-men squeal with fearful victory.

One last pull – all hands sprawl backwards –
the winning team. BlackBird staggers and drags
to freedom at the cost of his beak –
held fast by the hooks. His face is flat
as a human face. He's bleeding, keening
as best he can from the hole where his beak's roots hang.

XV

We dug up that heap of old masonry.
Ripped out brambles, the white root of couch grass:
two pairs of hands, one eager, one less so.
We traced the stone's clean lines in the earth.
Four inches, five, nine inches deep . . .
What forgotten treasure had we caught in the dirt?

A fluted column? As we scraped and clawed,
close-by, as firmly fixed in the same ground,
the white tip of something that after all
this time showed clearly, proud, its shaping lines.
Whatever it was – so carefully chiselled –
it most nearly resembled a feathery wing.

XVI

A channel we skipped through: *These are times
to try men's souls*. The world waited as Chris
stood on the brink of snow to wave me down.
What I wanted was a neatly swaying

planted pole, a hip-swing I imagined
like the sweeping pendulum in the Hong Kong Bank.

I zig-zagged across the slope, counting down
my real descent, while Chris waited below,
anonymous in goggles and hat, the bulk
of his jacket. Stationary, I knew
him by his colours. Moving, I knew his
individual rhythm, his lean amongst the rest.

I gravitated to him. The world watched.
What I wanted was not to seem anxious
and stiff, but skiers swooping by, a scratch-
sheet of ice, sudden deepening of snow,
slowly sapped my rhythm and my belief.
Frightened, I found I was drifting away from him.

I dug in hard – the world was waiting –
to correct my line – felt my weight simply
floating up from the slope – a wrong skyward
motion – left shoulder seeming now to lead –
for an instant – hanging – minutes – I have – long –
to plot the exact, criss-crossed patch of snow

where I have to fall – to pray my bindings
might burst or it would mean a busted leg –
or worse – something whacks my shoulder – wet snow
squeezes down my neck, inside my goggles,
scourges my left cheek and before I can feel
I have time to think: I've wiped-out. I'm still all right.

XVII

"He would have been dead by this time last night."
Carefully, we scraped around the white wing.
Side by side, each inside our private grief,
Chris swings towards me, easy, hunched.
I know him by his movement, his clothes.
Sliding to my crash-landing, he skis up the slope.

He spits feathers, cutting to a neat halt
where I lie. Looks down with a lovely grin.
"Why, Chris?" I'm yelling, "what the hell happened?
Didn't we understand each other once?
The years weren't worth one telephone call?
Your wife and child? You want to shrug them off?"

"It's an equation," he said, "of balance
and weight, speed and gravity – and you keep
getting it wrong. I'm sorry. Are you hurt?"
"Yes, I'm hurt. Don't joke. You want me to spell
it out?" I struggled onto one elbow,
pointed at him with the pole that clung to my wrist.

"Maybe you can't say. But I've guessed enough.
Your sweet maths won't stop inside computers.
It's deployed in the desert and you're afraid
I can't love you for that? Don't say it's drained
what little imagination you had?
What in the world has happened since I saw you last?"

XVIII

The slope curled up and slapped me to the ground.
His wife quickly said, "Chris has killed himself."
As I heard, she waited with the phone clamped
to her cheek, for the unnatural pause,
for the satellite's delay. "Killed himself.
And Andrew found him. On the upstairs bannister."

But he bends to me where I lie, crashed
in the snow. "Follow me, close as you can."
As he turns and is gone, I'm right on his
heels, moving as if I had never fallen.
BlackBird slinks off with the roots of his beak
hanging round his face like so much red spaghetti.

XIX

Chris suddenly cuts off the slope and I
follow as if I'm roped to him. BlackBird
filches a smock and fisherman's trousers.
He creeps to the long-house. His broken beak
lies, like a hat, a horn goblet. He grabs,
springs up and flies through the smoke-hole in the roof.

XX

We fly off-piste, past trees so close the sleeves
of my jacket scuff and snap the damp bark.
Then I'm stopped. Chris is quiet at my side.
"Put these on." A pair of old Smith goggles,
scratched and blurring. "I can't see anything."
"You asked what's happened since you caught that plane
    home."

The last thing I see are the snow crystals
melting on Chris's gloves as he brings them
up to my squinting eyes. Then frightened dark
as he wipes as if to clear the lenses –
we are still high up, but the mountain pines
have become the jumbled white roofs of a city.

Chris is at a window crossed with brown tape,
pointing at something that floats – a quiet
white cigar – across the rooftop, its tiny fins,
coming tame towards the Hotel. I scream,
knowing it will tear this place to the ground.
But what it has for a mind orders a right turn.

A dozen yards from us, obedient,
it sidesteps our building and gently drops
into the heart of a refinery
that burns all night. I think I see Chris smile.
For hours, we watch as the pale visitors
each turn their backs on us and slide to their targets.

XXI

Time ran out as we crossed the Hudson Bay.
I reached up and snapped out the reading-light.
Your family's fine but the children have colds,
meant it was going to happen. For real,
yellow flashes gaped in the horizon,
arcs of tracer fire squirted from the city roof.

XXII

Beneath the fisherman in a tall hat,
we gazed at BlackBird with his broken beak,
face no more than a ragged snout, features
bunched in a painful knot, cheeks arched
over the underlying broken bone,
clenching both wings like paws to his chest, like fists.

XXIII

I found Chris with a man in the lobby.
Avoiding my eyes, he talked, short and square,
how he, his boys owed their arses to Black-
Bird reconnaissance. How stealthed and immune,
they lock on the enemy, report, hand off.
Then he, his boys engage pursuit mode basically

till the ground is clear. How Pentagon's put
no flag on this play, so collateral's
likely since every damn mile's so target
rich. How it's a walk in the park. How most
shit kicked is enemy shit. Chris smiles, says:
"Remember Biggles? And Ginger? The Desert Rats?"

"I remember digging at a white wing.
I remember you losing interest
as you couldn't imagine what we'd found."
"Why," says Chris, "do you think I dragged you here?
So you can turn your tender back on this?
Don't say you get no kicks from this Boy's Own stuff.

If not the soldier in you – the scribbler?
The growth point of language is guns, not rhyme.
Didn't you sit goggle-eyed by the box
for weeks?" Again, his hands blanked out my eyes
till I heard a voice squalling *Gas! Gas! Gas!*
So easily, drawing a gun from the holster

on my hip, I snatch the respirator's
plastic green hood. I'm chanting, *Be'n time.*
Do it in nine. Stay 'live, do it in five.
We wheeze through long beaky snouts for an hour.
My amplified breath reminds me how
fragile is the unconscious rhythm of my lungs.

XXIV

A hoarse klaxon blows. False alarm this time
(a tank's exhaust set the detector off) –
"But next time?" Chris asks, turns quickly away,
goes to stand as usual at the snow-brim.
I see we have not left the mountain-side.
Again, I try to wipe my goggles clear for good.

XXV

BlackBird – even with his beak restored –
(he's tied it in place with fisherman's twine)
is still hungry after the energy
expended in his wounding. He hides
near the village of halibut fishers.
Shuts his bleary eyes to consider the options.

XXVI

I raise my gloves as if I might weep.
Refocussing, a man tugs at Chris's arm.
"Listen, how the boy spends night after night
in shelter and says he's almost happy,

watches videos of Eastwood, Bruce Lee
on the patched-up generator, an old TV.

Everything flashes fire as one comes down
the vent. Now we each run to the shelter,
where there is a smoking oven that takes
a day to cool. Go in. There is nothing
in the blankets that can be carried out."
At what he cannot see, Chris sits in the snow.

XXVII

At that instant, the low Pacific clouds
that drift around Whistler broke below us.
Where they opened, we could see a city,
glittering white beneath the tar-black smoke
that bellied up from many orange fires
like scattered gouts of fat across a tablecloth.

Threading towards us, a highway vanished
beneath the mountain's foot. We stood beside
its pocky tarmac. Sunlight. A grid-lock
of luxury saloons, jeeps, trucks, stalled
fire engines, a bulldozer. Any set
of wheels seemed to have been rashly commandeered to

drive into the red heart of a firestorm,
fierce enough to scald the windshield glass to gobs
of silicone. That there were survivals
at all was a miracle: a new case
of White Flake laundry soap, slightly burned.
A black bird face-down, is Donald Duck turned up.

A glossy calendar – some daffodils,
thatch, white café tables, a tall skyline.
I saw a squeezed tube of toothpaste, saying
(it was a dream) this jam's not deserted –
it has been stopped dead. I scraped off more
soil: the wing met the column as I knew it would.

XXVIII

Closer. Each of the cabs sheltered black loads,
shapeless at first, the colour of weathered
coal, the texture of a sooty coral.
Memory releasing, I recognised
what had been teeth – these grinning because
the lower jaw and face-bottom had been torn off.

In the flat bed of a stalled Nissan truck,
this coal-shape went head-down, hopeful ostrich,
its buttocks arrested in mid-air, legs
blasted at mid-thigh, ending abruptly
in a flutter of charcoal like the film
of carbon it must have watched in a childhood fire.

In the Ford ahead, a creature's body
has been blown open, double-doors onto
organs neatly packed, cooked to ebony.
In a Renault van, a squat roughened log.
A shell-wound like a knot-hole in its chest.
I think of the minutes Chris and I scraped soil,

cleaning our two-winged treasure, our flurry
of pleasure, greed and – I remember now –
frightened my imagination might
not prove true. Between the V of wings, we
found its beakless head – tiny and fragile –
but hidden, clogged with dirt, so we pulled it loose.

Earth, clay and roots, still cloaked what we had,
so we lugged it to the water-butt –
almost dropping it as we ran and plunged
it deep. Brown soil clouds began to blossom
and blind. Now we scraped and rubbed and probed
and almost wet ourselves in anticipation,

the water slopping muddy up our arms.
Then we stopped dead — four hands under water,
a blanked surface — sure our find was clean
beneath the murk. We looked at each other.
Counted down and four marbley-cold hands hauled
the weight of a strange, white bird into daylight,

hiked above water, our heads — a stone angel,
pale and dribbling silver in the daylight.
I was sick over and over beside
the highway. Chris stared. "Has no-one explained
the ugliness of war?" "So this is why?"
Careful, I edged to the brink of snow where he sat.

"At least," I said, tugging his thick jacket
with one gloved hand, "at least you've explained
how to make sense of your death. This degree
of horror . . . the guilt . . . the things we've seen
are not supportable — how this cheapness
of human life might become irresistible . . ."

"Don't get me wrong," Chris says, for the first time
seeming angry. "I've made too little sense
from beginning to end, although I guess
when we stand on Whistler in snow and sleet,
we pattern what happens in the desert.
This hand's yours. Some other's guilt is no proof

of innocence and to forget that defines
what's wrong. And this" — waving a hand to where
the highway had been — "was some sort of good
against evil thing that could not be ignored.
I've shown you to prise you out of your books.
I've shown you so you appreciate your brother's

imagination." "But you took your life . . ."
"Nothing so simple, my little brother.
Remember one day we dug up an angel
and dropped it in water and held it up?

112

That was the last simple thing in the world.
Don't depend on it, little brother, it won't do."

XXIX

BlackBird pondered and then finally thought
he knew what to do. He squeezed himself
into a smaller and human form, strode
to the village of halibut fishers
who all welcomed home this strong young stranger
and they promptly sat him at a table to eat.

XXX

Chris had already gone down the snow trail.
I only knew him by his rhythm, his clothes.
(Side by side, each in our private grief.)
He reached the foot of the mountain before
I'd begun. Now I looked for his advice.
"Look up. Lean out of the slope. Plant. And punch."